OPERATION
ART

Contents

Introduction

[Paul said,] **"My purpose is that they may be encouraged in heart and united in love, so that they may have the full riches of complete understanding, in order that they may know the mystery of God, namely, Christ, in whom are hidden all the treasures of wisdom and knowledge"** (Colossians 2:2–3).

God's great love for us is indeed a wonderful mystery! After all, who can understand how God could love us sinners so much that He would send His one and only perfect Son, Jesus, to suffer and die in our place? Who can fathom the depth of His great love and the richness of His treasures of eternal life, forgiveness, peace, joy, and hope that He gives us in Christ?

God reveals the mystery of Jesus to us through His love letter to the world—the Bible. As God leads us to be "detectives of Scripture," the Holy Spirit helps us to know Jesus better and better.

This book of crafts, puzzles, and game ideas is meant to give young detectives of God's Word additional ways to investigate the wonders of God's love for them. By exploring with art and craft materials, many directly from God's natural creation, the message of God's love for them in Jesus will be reinforced and applied to their lives in creative and meaningful ways.

This book includes five sections: **Garden Investigations; Mountain Investigations; Temple Investigations; Investigating God's Treasures;** and **Investigator's Index** which includes bulletin board and other craft ideas tied directly to a detective theme.

These crafts, puzzles, and games are supplements to the 1995 Concordia VBS course, *God's Special Agents: Discovering Jesus in the Bible.* But they can also stand alone as part of summer Sunday school or year-round craft activities. Learning center ideas to enhance your craft area are depicted on the title page for each section of the book. Use these suggestions to make special detective stations in your classroom.

You'll note that each activity includes an age group recommendation, indicated by a number within the magnifying glass at the top of each page. For example, 6 followed by an arrow pointing upward indicates the project would be most suitable for children ages 6 and up. These age designations will help as you select projects and puzzles for the students in your congregation.

May you share God's love with one another and with others as you use the ideas in this book.

The Author

God Made Me Fingerprint Magnets

Evidence

Thin, 2″ to 3″ diameter wooden hearts
Magnetic strips (self-adhesive)
Acrylic paints and brushes
Washable, nontoxic ink stamp pads (dark-colored) or
    tempera paint
Paper towels
Black fine-point markers
Paint smocks
Hairdryer (*Optional*)

Clues

1. Have the students put on paint smocks to protect their clothing from acrylic paints.
2. Paint the wooden hearts on both sides. Let these air dry or dry with a hairdryer.
3. Press a thumbprint on the center of a heart using the ink stamp pad or tempera paint. Have some wet and dry paper towels on hand so the students can wipe off their thumbs when finished.
4. When thumbprints are dry, write Christ-centered messages around the outer areas of the heart.
5. Attach a magnetic strip to the back of the heart for use as a refrigerator magnet.

Optional: Have each student make three hearts. Glue the finished hearts onto small grapevine wreaths. Add a narrow satin ribbon bow to complete.

Deductions

Discuss how God has created each one of us as special and unique. One way our uniqueness is shown is in our thumbprints. God loves each one of us as His own precious individual. Even if *you* were the only sinner on earth, God would still have sent Jesus to be *your* Savior. That's how much He loves you!

Bible readings: **Genesis 2 and 3; Psalm 139:13–16**

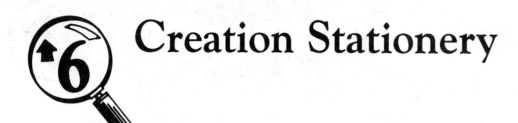

Creation Stationery

Evidence

White typing paper
White envelopes (4⅛″ × 9½″)
Washable ink stamp pad or tempera paint (dark colors)
Fine-point markers

Clues

Note: If you use tempera paint for the fingerprints, premix it to a thick consistency. Use small margarine containers to mix your paint.

1. Invite the students to choose a corner of a piece of paper. Have them place their thumbprint in their chosen corner.
2. Give them fine-point markers and invite them to design an animal or human face and body within their thumbprints. Fish, mice, owls, and ladybugs are but a few possibilities. Encourage the students to design people and animals which God created rather than monsters or other imaginary creatures.
3. Use the fine-point markers to print a Bible verse or other message across the bottom or top of the stationery to share God's love. Suggestions: **God is love. (1 John 4:16)** or **We love because He first loved us. (1 John 4:19)**
4. Make an envelope to match the stationery using the thumbprint creature idea.

Deductions

Discuss the uniqueness of God's animal and human creations. (See **Genesis 2** and **3**.) Invite the students to write a note on the stationery to witness to God's love for them in Christ Jesus. Send the note to a friend or relative. Purchase stamps so that the students can mail their letters.

Hands to Work/Hearts to God Wall Hanging

Evidence

Tan or other light color burlap, cut into 9″ × 12″
  rectangles (for small hands), or 15″ × 18″
  (for larger hands)
Poster paint
Large Styrofoam meat trays or shallow baking pans
  (for holding paint and dipping hands)
Newspaper
Fabric paint (preferably dark or bright colors in
  squeeze bottles with fine-line tips; Tulip brand)
Dowels for hanging
Cord, string, or yarn (25″ lengths)

Clues

1. Precut the burlap into sizes that amply allow
   space for the students' hand prints.
2. Cover the work area with newspaper. Place the
   burlap pieces onto the work space horizontally.
3. Have each child dip his or her hands into the
   paint. Be sure the student holds his or her hands
   stiffly. Make sure the palm surface of each hand
   is completely covered with paint.
4. With hands stiff, have each child lay his or her
   hands onto the center of the burlap piece.
5. Wipe each child's hands with paper towels, then
   wash thoroughly.
6. When the hand prints are dry, add the words
   Hands to Work, Hearts to God around the hand
   prints using the squeezable fabric paint. Leave
   about two inches at the top of the banner for use
   later. Also print the child's name in the bottom
   right-hand corner of the banner.
   Note: You will have to do this printing for
   younger children. Students age seven and up can
   do their own printing. You might print the words
   on the chalkboard or poster for them. Let them
   practice using the squeeze bottles on a separate
   piece of cloth to get the feel of the painting
   before they print the words on the banner.
7. When the paint is dry, cut slits about one inch
   apart at the top of the burlap. Weave the dowel in
   and out of the slits. Tie a length of cord or string
   to each end of the dowel to hang.

Deductions

If students haven't already noticed, point out the
heart shape formed in the center of each hand print.
After Adam and Eve's sin, God told Adam he would
have to work hard on the earth (**Genesis 3:23**). We
use our hands now as we work for God. Also discuss
how God helps us to serve Him and to serve others
with our hands. We serve God as a result of and a
response to the love and faith God gives us.

Discuss ways that you and your students can use
your hands and hearts to serve God. Make plans to
carry out one of the ways you mention.

Fruit Secrets

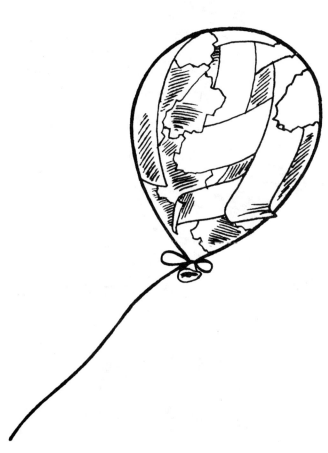

Evidence

Small balloons (one per child)

Strips of newspaper (about ½" wide)

Homemade flour or wheat paste, mixed to the consistency of cream

Shallow aluminum pans

Small pieces of typing paper (1" × 3") for secret messages

String for tying and hanging balloons

Orange, yellow, green, and red tempera paint

Bent paper clips or ornament hangers

Clear acrylic spray or varnish for protecting tempera paint finish

Clues

1. Have each child write a secret message (Bible verse, message of God's love, or one word each from a Bible verse you have selected) onto a small piece of paper.

2. Give each child a balloon. Have students roll up their secret messages and slip them inside the balloons. Help the children as necessary to blow up their balloons, and knot or tie the end. (*Option*: The teacher can also make messages ahead of time and place them in the balloons. Then tie and inflate the balloons ahead of time as well. The messages will truly be a mystery to the children if you choose this option.)

3. Pour the flour paste you have prepared into shallow pans. Show the students how to dip the newspaper strips into the paste until saturated. Also show how to remove the strips and wipe off excess paste by gently pulling the strips between the fingers. Then help the students as necessary to place the wet strips onto the inflated balloons. Cover all but the top ½ inch near the tied part of the balloon so that the message can be removed easily.

4. Hang the wet papier-maché balloons on hooks to dry overnight. *Note:* Drying may take several days in humid areas.

5. When the balloons are dry, paint them in colorful fruit colors using the tempera paint.

6. When the "fruit" is dry, pop the balloons with a sharp pin or an unfolded paper clip. Remove the secret messages. See "Deductions" for sharing ideas. After the balloons are popped, place a bent paper clip or an ornament hanger inside the top of the fruit to hang.

Deductions

If you have placed one word from a Bible verse into each balloon, let the students work together as a class to put their discovered messages together in the correct order.

If students have designed their own messages, let them trade their fruit with another student. Each student will reveal the others' messages.

Or have students prepare fruit and messages. Then share these with another class or with people in a retirement center or nursing home.

Or preprint numbered clues for a treasure hunt and place these inside the fruit. When the students pop the balloons and pull out the clues, work together to find the treasure (perhaps a picture of Jesus for each child to take home or small crosses, etc.).

Tie-Dye Snake

Evidence

White T-shirts (one per child)
Fabric dye (bright colors)
Plastic spray bottles
Rubber bands
Newspaper
Paint smocks

Clues

Note: Machine wash and dry the T-shirts before beginning this project.

1. Have each child put on a paint smock to protect his or her clothing from the fabric dye. Also cover your work area and floor with newspapers.
2. Roll up each T-shirt on the diagonal and fold each diagonal roll in half as shown in the illustration.
3. Bind the two halves together using rubber bands as shown. Space the rubber bands differently on each T-shirt so that each shirt's design will be a little different. (The mystery will be revealed when the shirt is unrolled!)
4. Prepare the fabric dye according to package directions. Pour the dye of various colors into separate spray bottles. Let the children spray the different colors onto the T-shirts at the rubber-banded areas. Let the dye dry completely.
5. Remove the rubber bands and unroll the T-shirts to see the design made by the dye and the rubber bands. Wear the T-shirts as a reminder of the joy we have because Jesus has conquered sin and death for us forever!

rolled up shirt

folded and rubber banded

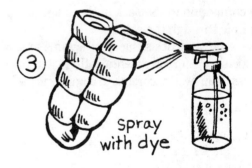

spray with dye

Deductions

The rolled-up shirts look like the shape of a snake. Show this shape as you review the Bible story in **Genesis 3.** When the students unroll their finished T-shirts, note how the body and arms of the T-shirt form a cross shape. The cross reminds us that God sent Jesus as the promised Savior to suffer and die for our sins and to rise triumphantly for us. The bright colors and patterns on the finished shirts remind us of the joy we have in Jesus' resurrection.

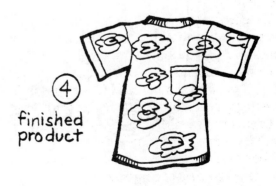

finished product

Garden of Eden Necklace

Evidence

Oven-baked modeling compound (Fima or Sculpey)
Cookie sheets
Spatula
Narrow ribbon
Toothpicks
Acrylic paint (unless you use colored modeling compound)
Fine-point bristled paint brushes
Paint smocks
Newspaper

Clues

1. Shape the following items out of small pieces of the modeling compound: a serpent, a tree, a piece of fruit (not necessarily an apple), Adam, Eve, a cross, and 12 round beads. See the illustrations for sample figures. *Note*: If working with younger children, it may be helpful to draw these patterns on the chalkboard or large piece of paper to help them visualize as they sculpt.
2. Poke a hole from side to side through the center of each shape. See the illustration. If the shape is too small to pierce, add a small square of modeling compound to the back of the shape and place the hole through the square.
3. Place each student's shapes in the same area of the cookie sheets for easy identification later. Bake the shapes in an oven according to compound package instructions. It usually takes about 20 minutes in a 275 degree oven to fully bake. Remove shapes from the oven and cookie sheet with a spatula and let them cool.
4. If you are not using colored compound, paint the figures using acrylic paint. The students may want to use black paint to highlight and give detail to the figures. Let the paint dry.
5. String the figures onto the ribbon as shown in the illustration. Place two round beads between each figure. Tie as a necklace.

Deductions

Use this necklace as a witnessing tool to tell the story of our sin and our salvation through Jesus. Base your storytelling on the facts from **Genesis 3** and also on the crucifixion accounts in the Gospels.

Mystery Word Search 1

(Based on **Genesis 3**)
Solution on page 62.

GOD
GARDEN
EDEN
TREE
SERPENT
EVE
FRUIT
WISDOM
SIN
ADAM
FIG
CHERUBIM
SWORD
GENESIS

Mixed-up and Mysterious Animals

Evidence

Drawing paper
Markers, colored pencils, crayons
Sample photographs of animals (see coloring books, *Ranger Rick* or *National Geographic* magazines, or other nature magazines)

Clues

1. On drawing paper, invite each child to draw a picture of a mixed-up animal. Let the children look at the pictures of real animals you have gathered, to choose body parts as they design their own mysterious animal. For example, a mixed-up animal might have the trunk of an elephant, the stripes of a zebra, the neck of a giraffe, the body of fish, and the spikes of a porcupine.
2. Encourage the children to use bright colors and lines and designs as they draw their mysterious animal. Also let them think of a name for their animal. It might be a compilation of name parts of the real animal on which their mixed-up animal is based. Or it might be a totally new name.

Craft variation: Let the students cut up their pictures into puzzles (four to five pieces each). Then invite them to trade their pieces with a friend. Work to put together the other person's mixed-up and mysterious animal.

Deductions

Invite willing students to share their creations. Then talk about the wonderful way in which God actually created the animals. Emphasize that God knew exactly what each animal would need to live and that's why He made them the way He did. God's creation was perfect.

Bible reading: **Genesis 1:20–25**

God's Wonderful World Booklet and Litany

Evidence

12″ × 18″ construction paper
Thick craft glue (such as Tacky)
Nature materials: seed pods, grass, dried flowers, leaves, twigs, fallen flowers, pebbles
Arts and crafts odds and ends: sandpaper, glitter, chenille wires, fabric scraps, rickrack, feathers, silk flowers, buttons, wiggly eyes
Crayons
Watercolor paints and brushes
Water containers
Colored chalk
Markers
Tissue paper
Paper punch
One large binder ring

Clues

1. Following your discussion of the creation story, **Genesis 1** and **2,** ask the students what their favorite thing is that God created. As the children name items, list them on the chalkboard or large piece of paper.
2. After the students have named their favorite items, let them use the materials you have gathered to make a picture of their item on the construction paper. Guide children to use ideas that fit their choice. (For example, a beach with rocks and sandpaper; watercolor for the ocean.) You might take children on a nature walk so they can gather items for their pictures.
3. Glue the desired items to the construction paper to form the picture. Use paint, crayons, colored chalk, and markers to add to the pictures. *Note*: As the children work, make sure they leave a one-inch space at both the top and bottom of their papers for the litany part of this activity.
4. When the pictures are complete and dry, gather the children together with their pictures to write the litany. Ask each child to name their pictured item. Place their named item in this phrase: **Thank You God for (fish).** Print this sentence at the top of the picture. Then ask the child, **Why are (fish) so wonderful?** Print the child's response at the bottom of the picture. For example, **Fish can swim gracefully. They have beautiful colors and patterns.** If you are working with students ages 7 and up, they can write their own sentences on their pictures.
5. Punch a hole in the upper-left corner of each picture. Bind the pictures into a booklet using the binder ring.
6. As you turn the pages, have the children read the litany together with you. Pray this during your closing worship time.

Deductions

The application value of this craft is built into its directions. Encourage older students to share their class book and prayer with a class of younger students, with nursing home residents, or as part of a Sunday morning worship service. It is a wonderful way to thank and praise God for His wonderful creation!

Bible readings: **Psalm 148; Psalm 104:1–28**

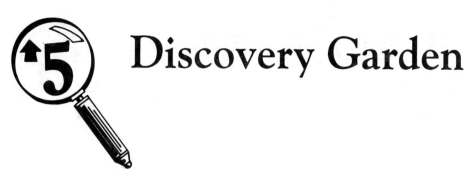

Discovery Garden

Evidence

Glass pie plate
Small pieces of brick
Plastic container for mixing ingredients
4 Tablespoons water
4 Tablespoons liquid bluing
4 Tablespoons iodized salt
1 Tablespoon ammonia
Several drops of food coloring
Newspaper

Clues

Note: If you teach younger students, you will want to mix and pour the chemicals yourself. If you teach older students, let them assist you with the measuring and mixing.

1. Cover the work area with a thick layer of newspaper.
2. Place the pieces of brick into the glass pie plate.
3. Mix the water, liquid bluing, salt, ammonia, and food coloring in a plastic container. Pour the mixture over the bricks in the pie plate.
4. The brick and chemical mixture will begin to produce crystals in just a few hours.

Deductions

As you pour the chemicals over the bricks, have the students use their detective skills to note how these materials look. Have them use these skills again as they compare these first descriptions to how the brick garden looks later when the crystals begin to grow. Then talk about how, through Christ Jesus, God has transformed us ugly sinners into His beautiful, forgiven people. As you note the changes in the garden from beginning to end, note how God changes us (God forgives our sins; He cleanses our hearts; He enables us to live for Him).

Bible readings: **2 Corinthians 5:17; Hebrews 9:14**

Mystery Beads

Evidence

Per student:

Two crimp beads (found in jewelry sections of craft stores)
Pliers
Fishing line or thin monofilament
Beads (see hand sizes for amounts as listed below)

For a small hand:
  33 4mm colored beads
  163 4mm white beads

For a medium hand:
  33 4mm colored beads
  205 4mm white beads

For a large hand:
  33 4mm colored beads
  253 4mm white beads

Clues

1. Cut a piece of fishing line or monofilament two feet long for each student.
2. Place a small crimp bead at one end of the fishing line. Squeeze it tightly shut with the pliers. This will hold the other beads in place on the line.
3. String the correct number of beads according to the pattern below. Work down the columns from left to right until you finish the last column. *Note:* You might want to give each student a copy of the pattern, or print it out on the chalkboard or large piece of paper so it can be easily read by all the students. Or string the beads in sets as a class to avoid confusion (Have everyone string the first 14 white beads, then the four colored beads, and so on.)

w=white	c=colored	
14 w*	1 w	1 w
4 c	3 c	1 c
7 w	1 w	1 w
1 c	3 c	1 c
27 w*	27 w*	27 w*
1 c	1 c	4 c
10 w	2 w	1 w
1 c	1 c	3 c
27 w*	1 w	1 w
1 c	1 c	3 c
1 w	1 w	13 w*
2 c	1 c	1 c

* = for medium hands, add 7 white beads to total at each *
for large hands, add 15 white beads to total at each *

4. Place the other crimp bead on as close to the last bead as possible and squeeze it tightly shut with pliers.
5. Starting at the top of your fingers on the palm side of your hand and winding toward the other side of your hand, wrap the strung beads around your fingers to reveal the name of the person who is always with you. *Note:* The first four colored beads you strung should appear at the top side of your hand, on top of your index finger. See illustration.
6. The last colored bead on the string is just to distinguish the end of the string from the beginning.
   Wrapping hint: After wrapping around your hand, the next colored bead after the first 27 white beads should line up directly underneath the first colored bead. Each of the following one colored beads should continue to line up.

Deductions

This craft demonstrates the great mystery that, although we cannot see God, we know that He is always with us. Do not tell the students why they are stringing the beads in the pattern shown. Let the pattern reveal itself when the students wind the beads around their fingers.

Detective Discovery Rebus

Evidence

Heavy stock white paper
White crayons
Watercolor paints, brushes, water containers
Newspaper
Paint smocks

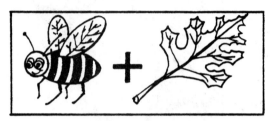

BE LIEVE

Clues

1. Cover your work area with newspapers. Have students wear paint smocks to protect their clothing.
2. Give each student (or pair of students) a piece of paper and a white crayon. Invite them to think of a rebus-type coded message that tells something about Jesus or that depicts a Bible story or Bible verse. Have them draw their rebus message on the paper using the white crayon.
3. Exchange papers with one another. Provide watercolor paints, water, and brushes. To reveal the hidden rebus message, have the students paint over the paper with the paints using a dark color.
4. Take turns decoding and reading the revealed messages.

LOVE ONE ANOTHER

Deductions

This activity provides an excellent way for students to review Bible truths and Bible verses from their lessons. Older students could make simple messages for younger children to paint and decode. This also could be a fun way for students to witness to other students about Jesus using messages that describe Him and His love.

Detective Focus

Find at least five differences between these two garden pictures. Circle the differences you find in the picture at the bottom of the page.

Son Wreath

Evidence

Per student:

30 pieces of yellow plastic (from newspaper bags or colored trash bags); each piece 4″ × 6″
Scissors
12″ yellow pipe cleaner
Glue (Thick craft glue and thinner white school glue)
Fabric paints, glitter paints, permanent markers (*optional*)

Clues

1. Cut the plastic strips before class, especially for younger students. Place each set of 30 strips in a plastic bag for each child.
2. Form a circle with the pipe cleaner and twist the ends together. Make a small circle or hook with any pipe cleaner remaining at the end so that the finished craft can be hung in a window.
3. Fold one of the plastic strips in half and lay it over the edge of the pipe cleaner. Bend the unfolded ends underneath the pipe cleaner and up through the loop formed by the folded end of the plastic strip. This will make a knot like those used in rug hooking.
4. Continue in this manner with the remaining strips until the pipe cleaner circle is covered.
5. Trim the remaining ends of the strips so that they are even. Fluff out the plastic for a full appearance.
6. Using a remaining plastic strip, cut a circle to fill the opening of the wreath. Glue this circle in the center of the wreath using a thick craft glue applied to the back side.
7. On the front, in the center of this plastic circle, make a small cross using thin white glue. Make sure the wreath lays flat until the glue cross has dried clear.
8. Hang the finished wreath in a window with lots of light. As the sun shines through the wreath, the cross will appear in the center of the wreath.

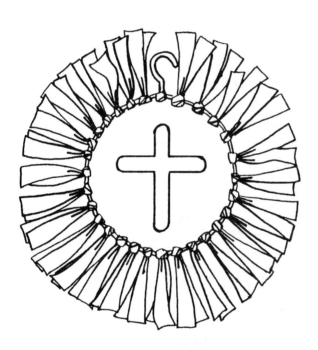

Deductions

This wreath is a visual reminder of Jesus, God's Son, our Savior. As the cross appears only when light shines through the wreath, this adds an air of discovery to the craft.

As you make this craft, discuss how God sent Jesus into the world to save us from the darkness of sin. God first promised Jesus to Adam and Eve. Jesus died and came alive again for us. He is the Light who has conquered the darkness of sin and death for us forever.

As this craft uses recycled materials, it is a good one to use when talking about the care of God's creation. See **Genesis 1:28–30.** Bible readings: **John 8:12; John 12:46; 1 John 1:5–7**

Pebble Search

(Based on an ancient Egyptian game)

Evidence

15 pebbles per game set
Sandwich-size reclosable plastic bags to keep pebbles
in or small drawstring cloth bags

Clues

1. Place the pebbles in a horizontal row. Have one
   student sit on each side of the row.
2. Decide who will go first. The first player takes one,
   two, or three pebbles.
3. Play continues with the second player taking one,
   two, or three pebbles. No more than three pebbles
   can be taken by a player on his or her turn.
4. The object of the game is to be the player to take
   the last pebble. The strategy comes in as each player decides how many pebbles to take on each turn.
   The student will want three or fewer pebbles to
   remain on his or her last turn so that he or she
   can take the last one.

Deductions

This is a good game to sharpen your young agents'
detective skills.

For younger children: Hold an odd or even number
of pebbles in your hand. Ask the children to guess the
number of pebbles you hold. The pupil who guesses
correctly gets to hold the pebbles for the next round.

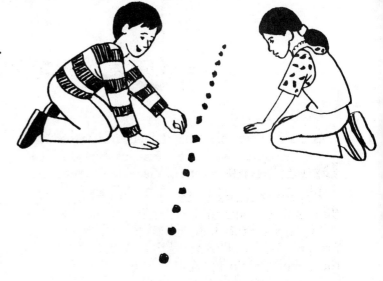

Ten Commandments Bookends

Evidence

Craft clay:
1 cup corn starch
2 cups baking soda
1¼ cup water (See recipe below.)

Large cooking pot
Several old cloths
Plastic bag
Old, dull pencils
Fleckstone spray
Felt

Clues

1. Before class, mix the corn starch, baking soda, and water together in a large cooking pot. Cook over medium heat until the mixture is thickened to a consistency of moist mashed potatoes. This consistency should occur about one minute after the mixture boils.
2. Remove the craft clay mixture from the cooking pot and let it cool under several damp cloths. When the clay is cool enough to handle, knead it to a modeling clay consistency. Store clay in a plastic bag until ready for use.
3. Give each student a workable amount of clay. Help them as necessary to mold and roll their clay into two shapes which resemble the Ten Commandments tablets. Make these tablets several inches thick so that they are free-standing. (See illustration.)
4. While the clay is still soft, etch shapes onto the front of each tablet using a dull pencil point. On one tablet, etch the shape of a heart with a cross superimposed on it. On the other tablet, etch the shape of a heart with a smiling face superimposed on it.
5. Lay these tablets flat to dry. Depending on the humidity in your area, this may take several days.
6. When dry, spray with Fleckstone according to package directions. This will give these tablets the appearance of granite. *An adult should do the spraying for pre-kindergarten and primary children.*
7. When dry, glue small pieces of felt to the bottom of the tablets to make them usable as bookends.

Deductions

As the students make their tablets, review the Ten Commandments together. See **Exodus 20:1–17.** The heart with the cross on one of the tablets reminds us that the first three commandments talk about how we are to honor and love God. The heart and smiling face on the second tablet remind us that the Fourth through Tenth Commandments focus on how we are to love others. Emphasize to the students that God gave us His commandments out of His love for us.

Mystery Word Search 2

(Based on **Exodus 19–20; 33–34**)
Solution on page 63.

```
FAJCB        FACBER
ATMADHF      COMIERC
NSIFSIYR    AHNCADSLC
MUQUMNEEAC  RIMJRTOKOO
OGDSEIXBOE  ADNORAAUSM
SRAWIATOST  DEPUOAKVEM
EMYTXNAVDA  INANSIMIPA
SABEGIADFB  AGLOMCNADN
ALENUSBIOF  NEXODUSSED
NEXIWEVYUN  TYLENZMOUM
TXTNANEVOC  HIECMBOYNE
BOADXTANDL  ETSONTNTON
STTUSCEKOB  MASCONLCNT
TECSUOMEAJ  OVAULSOPAS
EDDESERTAS  WEDREORTED
LUFRTVENIR  DYCSTQURTR
BNDANTZOMH  ELOAINCDQS
ALOPCAMSDM  EOUXCOMANT
TIMANESTMA  NBNIATNUOM
```

EXODUS
DESERT
MOSES
SINAI
CLOUD
MOUNTAIN
AARON
COMMANDMENTS
TABLETS
OBEY
COVENANT
RADIANT
FACE

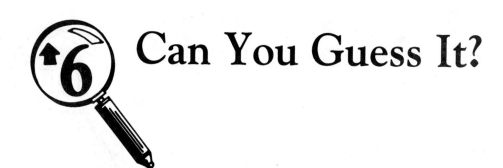

Can You Guess It?

Evidence

10 3" × 5" index cards (*Note*: If you have a large class, you may want to make more than one set of cards.)
Large hat or shoe box

Clues

1. Before play, print the Ten Commandments, one per card, on the index cards you have gathered. *Note*: The 1995 Concordia VBS Teachers Guides have some versions of the commandments in easier-to-understand language. See Lesson 2. Place the completed cards into a large hat or shoe box.
2. Divide your class into two or more teams. Decide which team will go first. A person from the first team will draw one of the commandment cards out of the hat or box. The team then has three minutes to work together to come up with a way to show their chosen commandment being followed in a positive way. No words can be spoken. Only actions can be used.
3. The team then presents their pantomime. The other team guesses which commandment is being acted out.
4. The other team then has a chance to select a commandment and to pantomime it. Play continues back and forth between teams until all the commandments have been chosen.

Deductions

This game is a way to review the Ten Commandments with your students. It is also a way for the students to think of and act out ways they can apply the Ten Commandments to their lives.

Rock Sculpting

Evidence

1 cup salt
1 cup flour
1 Tablespoon powdered alum
Large mixing bowl
Gallon-size resealable plastic bags
Large, clean Styrofoam meat trays
Old, dull pencils
Brown shoe polish or Fleckstone
White cotton rags
Newspaper

Deductions

As the children sculpt, talk about the strength and power Jesus showed when He kept God's Law perfectly for us and when He died and came alive again to conquer sin and death forever for us. The rock is a symbol of strength. We can depend on Jesus for all things. He promises to help us and to make us strong.

Bible readings: **Psalm 29:11; Isaiah 41:10; Philippians 4:13**

Clues

1. Before class, combine the salt, flour, and alum together in a large mixing bowl. Add water, small amounts at a time, until the dough is the consistency of putty. Place in plastic bags until ready for use.
2. Cover your work area with newspaper. Place a large amount of clay on a Styrofoam tray in front of each child. Invite the children to form their clay into large, bulky letters that spell *JESUS*. Make sure that each letter connects with the one next to it at several points so that the letters will dry together to form one unit. The students also can carve these letters into the dough mound with dull pencils, making crevices between each letter.
3. Let the dough dry overnight. Give each child a cotton rag with a very small amount of brown shoe polish on it. Show the children how to rub the shoe polish into the dried clay to give it a brown, wood-like stain.
4. When the shoe polish has been applied and rubbed in completely, give each child a clean cotton rag with which to buff the clay until it is clean to the touch. *Or, instead of using shoe polish, have an adult spray each carving with Fleckstone according to package instructions. Let dry completely.*

Gumshoe Rock Rubbings

Evidence

White drawing paper
Crayons
Rocks
Newspaper

Clues

1. Cover your work area with newspaper. Place a number of fairly flat, well-textured rocks on the newspaper.
2. Give each student a piece of paper and several crayons. Invite them to place their paper on top of a rock and rub the top of the paper with the side of the crayon point. The texture of the rocks will come through on the paper, making an interesting design.
3. *Note*: If your church has stone walls inside or outside, make rubbings from these walls. Take care not to leave crayon marks on these areas.
4. Use the rock rubbings as backgrounds for greeting cards, posters, stationery, or other uses you might discover.

Deductions

Use these rubbings as background paper for other art and craft projects which share Jesus with others. Crosses, hearts, butterflies, and other Christian symbols can be stenciled over these rock-rubbing backgrounds. Or print the Ten Commandments over the rock rubbings to make a poster the students can take home and display.

Gospel Bookmarks

Evidence

Mesh plastic canvas pieces, each cut into 6 holes × 21 holes (one piece per student)

1⁄16″ ribbon cut into 18″ lengths, one piece of each of the following colors per student: gray, red, white, blue, green, and gold

Clues

1. Turn the piece of plastic canvas so that the six-hole side is on the top. Tie the piece of gray ribbon tightly to the upper left corner of the plastic canvas.
2. Weave this gray ribbon in and out of the plastic canvas straight down the row until you reach the bottom. Avoid twisting the ribbon as you weave.
3. Tie the red ribbon in the second hole directly to the right of the gray ribbon. Weave the red ribbon in the same manner as described above to the bottom of the canvas.
4. Use the same process to weave the remaining colors of ribbon into the bookmark: white—third hole; blue—fourth hole; green—fifth hole; gold—sixth hole (farthest to the right).
5. Trim the bottom of the ribbons so they are the same length.

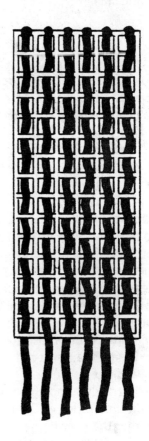

Deductions

Use this Gospel bookmark to tell others the story of what Jesus has done as our Savior. Explain that **gray is the color that reminds us of our sin. Red is the color of Jesus' blood, shed for us to take the punishment we deserved because of our sin. White is the color that represents our hearts now that they have been washed clean of sin by Jesus' death and resurrection. Blue is the color representing the faith that God gives** us in Jesus. **Blue is also the color that stands for truth. We can be certain that God's Word is true. Green is the color that reminds us of eternal life. We have eternal life because of Jesus. Gold is the color that reminds us of heaven. Someday we will live there with Jesus.**

The students can make several bookmarks to share with others.

Detective Decoder Wheel

Evidence

Card stock or old manila file folders
Pens and pencils
Scissors
Brads (one per student)
Thick elastic and stapler (*optional*)

Clues

1. Cut two circles from the card stock paper or file folders for each student. One circle should be 5" in diameter and the other 4" in diameter.
2. Mark the center of each circle by making a small dot with a pencil.
3. On the 5" circle, draw a light circular line 1" in from the edge around the entire circle. See Illustration 1.
4. On the inside of that pencil line, write the letters of the alphabet in order, spacing the letters as evenly as possible. See Illustration 2.
5. On the outside of the line, draw a symbol to represent each letter. Note that the symbol for each letter must be printed exactly across the circle from the letter it represents. See Illustration 3. Give younger students an established code to follow, perhaps the one illustrated. Older students can design their own code symbols, or use the suggested one.
6. Cut a small triangular notch out of the 4" circle as shown in Illustration 4. The notch should be slightly larger than one of the letters so that the letter will show from under the triangular cut.
7. Place the 4" circle on top of the 5" circle. With the tip of the brad, poke a small hole through the center of each circle as marked. Place the brad through these holes and fasten.
8. On the 4" circle, draw an arrow opposite the notched opening. See Illustration 4.
9. To code a message, turn the 4" circle until the needed letter is in the triangular opening. The arrow will then point to the corresponding symbol. To decode a message, turn the arrow until it points to the symbol and the corresponding letter will appear in the opening.

10. Divide the class into pairs of students, giving each pair a Bible, several index cards or sheets of paper, pencils, and their decoder wheels. Invite them to look up Bible verses they have learned and print them in code on the index cards or paper. Trade messages between pairs to decode. Print the decoded verses on the back side of the cards or paper.

Special variation for younger students: Turn the decoder wheels into decoder watches by fastening an elastic loop to the back of the fastened wheels with two small staples. Students can wear these on their wrists as they code and decode messages.

Deductions

Use these decoder wheels to give your students practice with Bible verses they have learned. Witnessing messages can also be devised and sent in code to share the Good News about Jesus with classmates and friends.

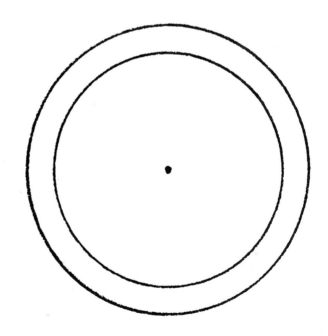

Illustration 1
5" circle

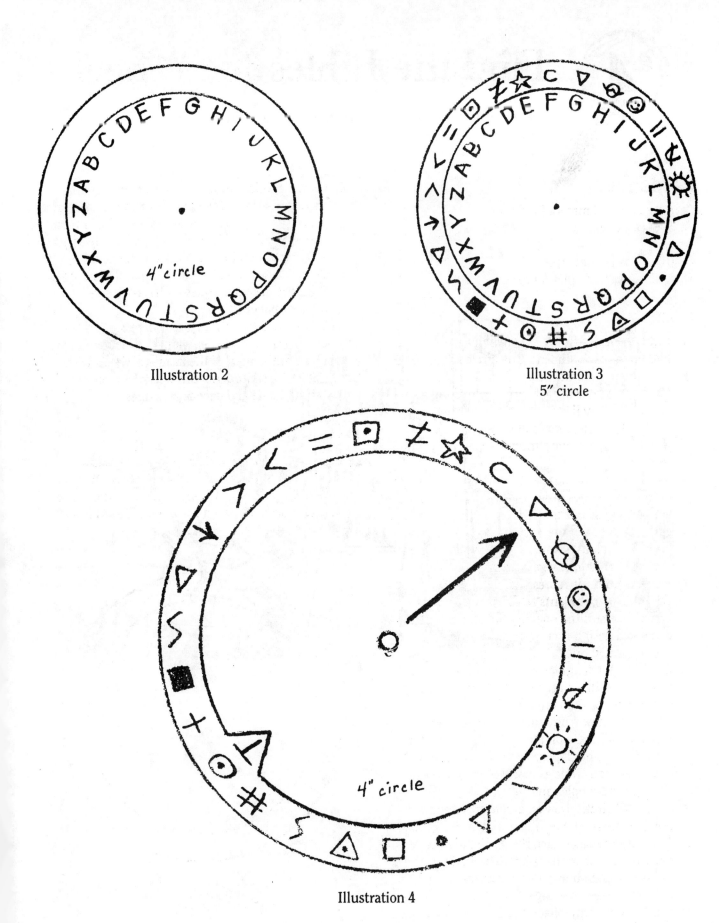

Illustration 2

Illustration 3
5" circle

Illustration 4

31

Find the Bibles

Use your detective skills to find five Bibles in this church library.
Circle each one you find.

Invisible Ink

Evidence

Milk
Small, shallow, empty, plastic margarine tubs
Cotton swabs
Blank 4″ × 6″ white index cards
Clothespins
Heat source (Use an iron, electric hot plate, or a high wattage light bulb in an open lamp base. Bulb must be higher than 100 watts.)

Clues

1. Pour a small amount of milk into a plastic margarine tub. Give each student an index card and a cotton swab.
2. Have the students dip their cotton swab into the milk and use it as a "pen" to write a message about God's love onto the card. Let the message dry completely.
3. Trade messages with a friend. Clip each message card onto a clothespin. **With the help and constant supervision of an adult, move the card evenly back and forth over the heat source, message side up. The invisible, secret message will soon appear.**

Deductions

Use this activity as a way for students to share Jesus' love with one another. It can also be used to review Bible verses or daily lesson truths.

The teacher can also prepare cards ahead of time using key words from the day's Bible story. As the key words reappear over the heat source, invite the students to tell the facts they remember about the Bible story.

Investigator's Bible Cover

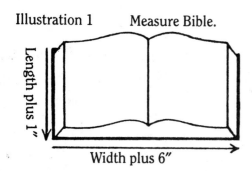

Illustration 1   Measure Bible.

Length plus 1"
Width plus 6"

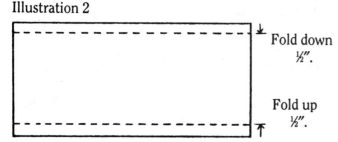

Illustration 2

Fold down ½".

Fold up ½".

Illustration 3

Rubber bands hold ← fabric on front → and back hardcovers.

Mark the center. ↑ Crease.

Illustration 4

Evidence

Bibles (one per student)
Rulers
Plain muslin or broadcloth
Rubber bands, ¼" thick (2 per student)
Squeezable fabric paint and/or fabric markers
Iron
Ironing board or thick pile of newspapers

Clues

1. Open the student's Bible and measure its entire length and the width of its cover. Add 6" to the width measurement and 1" to the length measurement. See Illustration 1. Follow these directions for any size Bibles your students bring.
2. Cut fabric to the size computed in direction 1 above.
3. Fold in the top and bottom edges of the fabric ½" each. Press flat to make hem. **Only adults should use the iron.** See Illustration 2.
4. Lay the Bible in the center of the iron-hemmed fabric. Slip rubber bands over the front and back hardcover of the Bible. See Illustration 3.
5. Fold 3" of each side of the fabric width over the front and back covers of the Bible and through the rubber bands. This will identify where the center of the Bible cover is. Make a small crease to mark the center and remove the fabric from the Bible.
6. Fold the fabric at the center. Use squeezable fabric paints or fabric markers to decorate the front cover of the fabric. Use Christian symbols and bright colors. See Illustration 4.
7. When the paint is dry on the front cover, the back can be painted as well.
8. When the paint is completely dry, place the fabric cover back over the Bible and through the rubber bands as explained in direction 5.

Deductions

As the students make their covers, talk about how the Bible is God's letter of love to everyone in the world. The Bible is the most important book we could ever read because it tells us about Jesus, our Savior. These Bible covers help identify our Bibles as precious to us.

Bible readings: **Psalm 119:105; John 17:17; 2 Timothy 3:15–17**

Mystery Verses

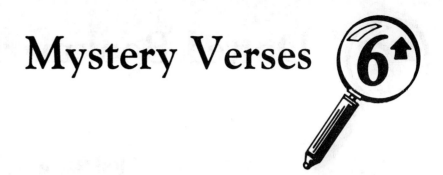

Evidence

3″ × 5″ plain white index cards
Waxed paper, cut into 4″ × 6″ pieces
Pencils
Bible

Clues

1. Use the "crayon resist" method for this activity. Place a piece of waxed paper over an index card.
2. Locate a favorite Bible verse in your Bible. Using the sharp point of a pencil, print this verse on the waxed paper, pressing firmly. The waxed letters transfer to the card if you press hard enough. Discard the waxed paper when you are finished.
3. Exchange cards with a friend.
4. To uncover the mystery verse, lightly rub the side of a pencil point back and forth across the waxy side of the index card. Your pencil rubbings will show on the unwaxed spaces of the card around all the letters. The wax of the letters will prevent the pencil rubbings from adhering, and the words will appear.

Deductions

Use this activity to practice Bible verses you have learned in your lessons. The students could also use this activity to send witnessing messages about Jesus' love to classmates and friends.

The teacher could make mystery verse messages ahead of time for the students to reveal in small groups. Or print a Bible verse, one word per card. After the students have revealed the words by doing pencil rubbings, have them work together to put the cards in correct verse order.

Dotted Bookmarks

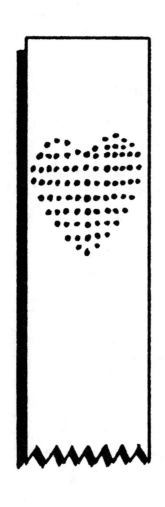

Evidence

Various bright colors of ribbon, 1½" to 3" wide
Scissors, regular and pinking shears
Graph paper
Pencils
Colorpoint paint stitching paints, dark colors

Clues

1. Cut the ribbon into 8" to 12" lengths. Angle edges, fringe, or cut with pinking shears.
2. Design a symbol or message with dots on graph paper using a pencil. Or follow the patterns provided on the facing page.
3. Transfer the design on to the ribbon using the Colorpoint paints.
4. Let the bookmarks dry overnight before using.

Deductions

   Share these bookmarks with others. Explain the symbols and what knowing Jesus means to you as you give the bookmarks as gifts. Purchase Bibles to send to relatives, friends, and people in other countries. Include a bookmark in each new Bible.

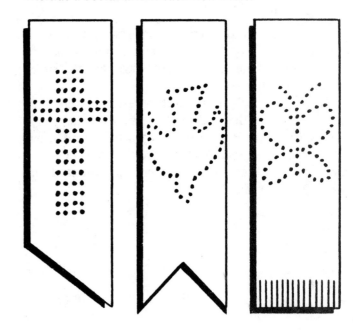

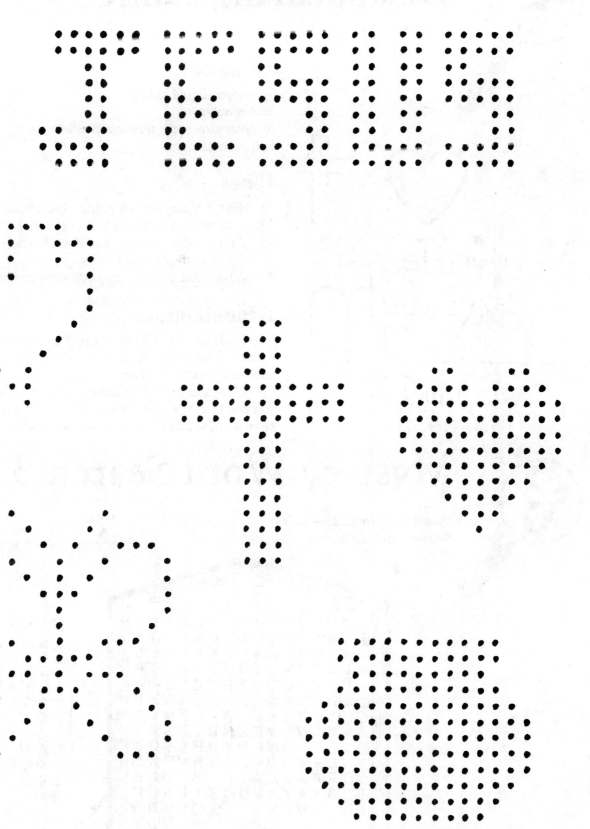

Disappearing Paint

Evidence

½ teaspoon liquid bluing
2 cups water
Medium-size empty plastic containers
Large paintbrushes

Clues

1. Mix the bluing and water in a plastic bowl.
2. Go outside to a smooth area of sidewalk. Paint Bible clues in rebus form on the sidewalk. These could also be in the form of riddles.
3. As the paint dries the message will slowly disappear.

Deductions

Use this activity as a fun way to share witness messages or Bible passages. Let the students solve one another's messages before they disappear.

Note: As this mixture is toxic, do not let children younger than age 5 participate in this craft. Carefully dispose of the paint mixture when you are finished.

Mystery Word Search 3

(Based on **2 Kings 22—23:25**)
Solution on page 63.

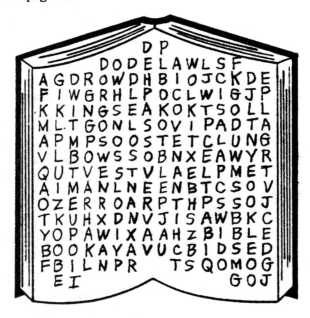

KINGS
TEMPLE
COVENANT
IDOLS
ALTAR
JOSIAH
LOST
BOOK
LAW
WORD
BIBLE
GOD

Special Agent Treasure Boxes

Evidence

Small hinged box or box with lid (2" × 3")
  Note: Plastic travel soap dishes with hinged lids also work well.
Craft sticks (Number needed per student will vary with size of box.)
Acrylic paints or permanent markers
Sequins, buttons, rickrack, fabric scraps
Thick craft glue
Newspaper
Clear strapping tape (*optional*)

Deductions

Fill your box with small cards on which are printed VBS Bible verses, mystery Bible messages, a small cross, or a small card with a picture of Jesus. Share the box of treasures with a friend. Tell your friend that your relationship with Jesus is your greatest treasure!

Clues

1. Cover the work area with newspaper. Turn the box over on its lid. Lay sticks horizontally across the box bottom to cover. Glue in place. Let dry slightly.
2. Turn the box over. Lay sticks on top of the box. Glue these in place.
3. When the lid is fairly dry, glue sticks to the front and back sides of the box to cover. Note that the ends of the box will remain uncovered. Leave a strip on the back area uncovered where the box is hinged so that the box will open and close easily.
4. When sticks are completely dry, use paint, sequins, and other materials you have gathered to decorate the boxes. Use Christian symbols such as hearts and crosses in the decorations. Magnifying glass outlines and question marks may also be included to emphasize the detective theme.

Note: If you use boxes with unattached lids, make a "hinge" for your box lid by placing a small piece of strapping tape partly on the box lid and partly on the back side of the box bottom.

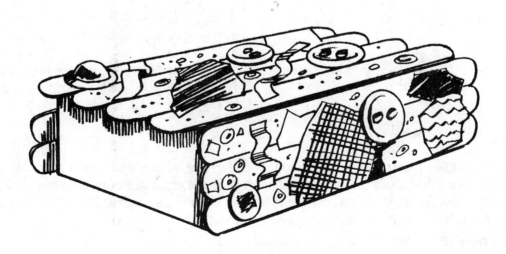

Surprise Treasure Box

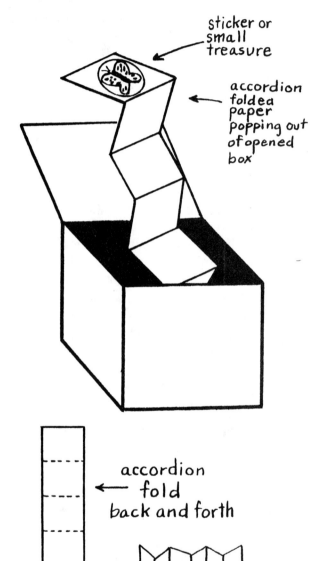

sticker or small treasure

accordion folded paper popping out of opened box

accordion fold back and forth

Evidence

Tagboard or old manila file folders
Box pattern (one per student; see facing page)
Adhesive tape
Glue
Construction paper
Scissors
Pencils
Markers
Small "treasures" (one per student): lightweight plastic cross, picture of Jesus, butterfly sticker, and so on

Clues

1. Duplicate a copy of the box pattern from page 41 for each student. Also gather your small treasures, perhaps from a local Christian bookstore.
2. Cut out the box pattern. Trace it onto the tagboard or manila file folders and cut out. *Note*: Have the pattern already traced and cut out of the tagboard for younger students.
3. Decorate the outside of the box using colorful markers. Use mysterious symbols such as question marks and arrows for decorations.
4. Assemble the box by folding the sides as indicated on the pattern. Fasten together with tape or glue.
5. Cut 1″ × 6″ lengths of construction paper, one per student. Accordion-fold these pieces of paper to make a spring. Glue one end of the spring to the inside bottom of the treasure box. Glue one of the treasures you have gathered to the other end. Gently suppress the finished spring and close the box lid.
6. To discover the surprise, pull the tab and gently squeeze the sides of the box. The lid will pop open, and the treasure will spring out!

Deductions

Invite the children to share their treasure boxes with a friend or family member. When the treasure pops out, help the children practice telling about the treasure: **Jesus died on the cross and came alive again for you. Jesus loves you and is your Savior. The butterfly reminds us of the new and eternal life Jesus gives us.** Formulate other statements based on the treasure you have placed in the box.

Bible readings: **Matthew 13:44; John 3:16; Ephesians 2:4–5; 1 John 3:16**

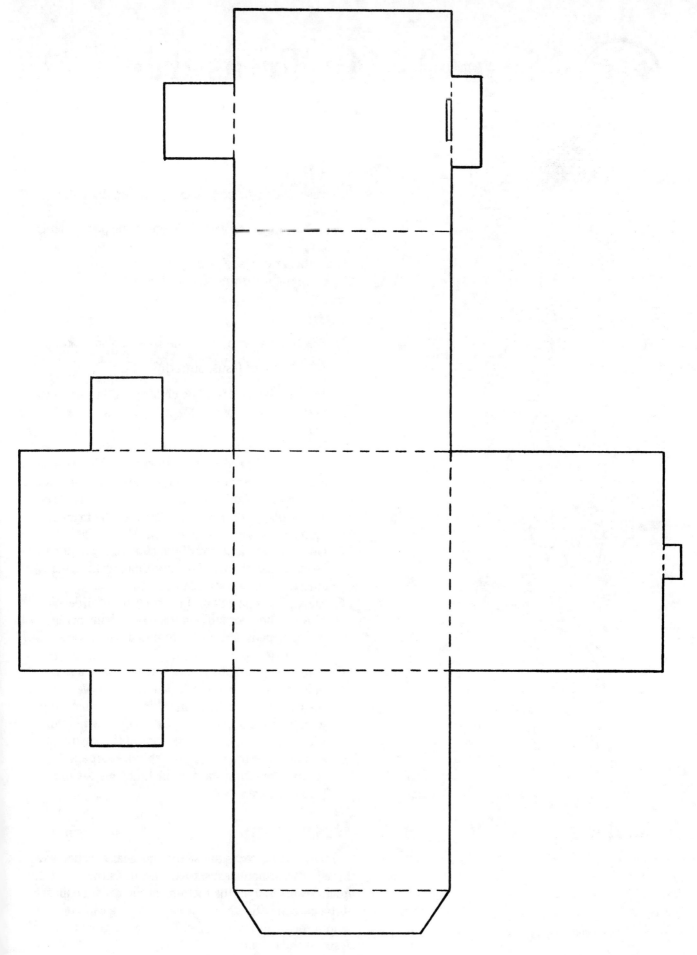

Jesus Is My Treasure-Surprise Spiral

Evidence

9″ circles of construction paper (one per student)
Scissors
1″ × 12″ strips of construction paper (one per student)
Markers
Small sticker of Jesus' face
Yarn, ribbon, or fishing line for hanger

Clues

1. Precut a circle for each child. Draw a spiral on it according to the pattern on page 43.
2. Give each child a circle you have prepared and a pair of scissors. Have the children cut a spiral out of the circle following the line you have provided. Set this aside.
3. Work together as a class to devise a list of qualities of Jesus based on the Bible stories you have studied. Some words you might include are: *Savior, loving, kind, Friend, Redeemer, God's Son, True God, True Man, Conqueror.* Print the words the children name on the chalkboard or large sheet of paper.
4. Give each student one of the construction-paper strips. Show them how to accordion-fold it, being sure to give each strip at least five folds.
5. Starting at one end of the strip, list four qualities of Jesus, one per fold, on the paper strips using marking pens. On the bottom fold, place the sticker of Jesus' face.
6. Using the point of a pair of scissors, poke a small hole in the top fold of the paper strip as well as in the center of the top of the spiral. Run a length of yarn, ribbon, or fishing line through the hole in the paper strip. Bring both ends of the string up and through the hole in the spiral. Knot and tape so that the string stays in the hole. See the illustration above.

Deductions

Invite the students to use this spiral as a visual way to tell others about Jesus, their Savior. As they read the qualities printed on the sections of the paper strip, see if the person with whom they are sharing can guess whom the qualities describe. Then reveal the picture of Jesus at the bottom.

Top view   Begin to cut here.

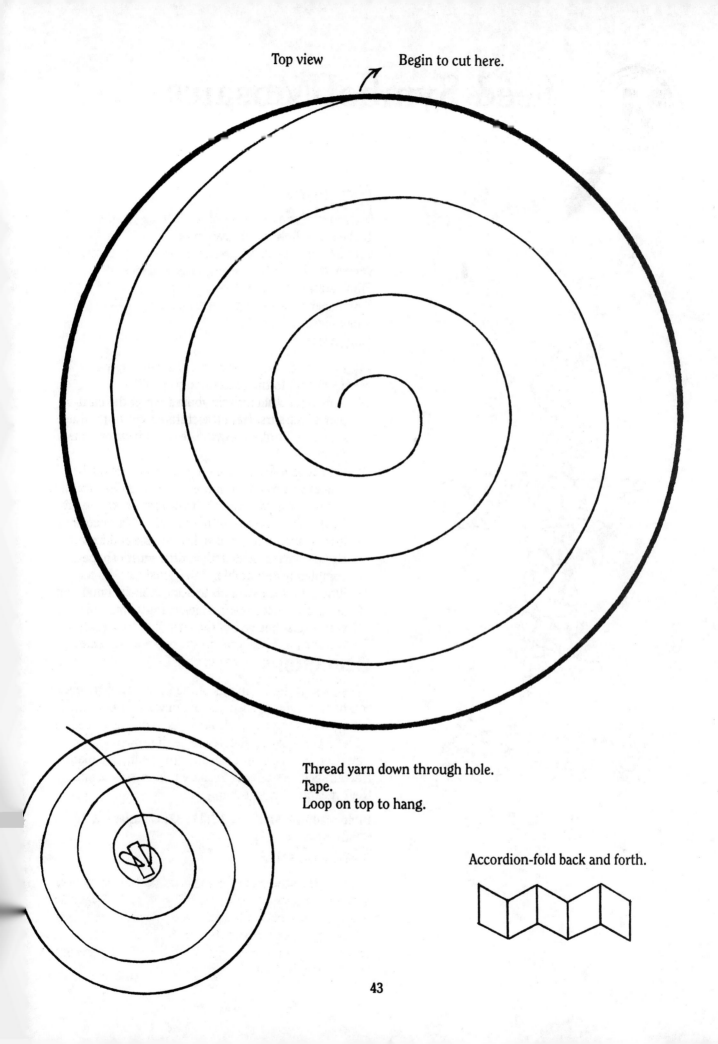

Thread yarn down through hole.
Tape.
Loop on top to hang.

Accordion-fold back and forth.

43

Seed Symbol Mosaics

Evidence

Tagboard or lightweight cardboard
Scissors
Variety of dried beans, seeds, peas, and rice
Thick craft glue
Newspaper
Small pieces of yarn
Adhesive tape

Clues

1. Before class begins, cut shapes out of the cardboard using the stencil patterns on page 45, one shape per student. Cover the work area with newspaper.
2. Let the students choose one of the Christian shapes you have cut out. Demonstrate how to fill in the shapes by first covering a small area of the shape with a thin layer of craft glue. Then cover this area using the seeds, beans, and other materials you have provided. Cover the entire shape as completely as possible.
3. When the seed symbols are dry, make a loop hanger on the back of each shape using a small piece of yarn and adhesive tape.

Deductions

Talk about the meanings of the Christian symbols you have provided. Then discuss how God helps our faith grow as the Holy Spirit works in our hearts when we hear God's Word. Relate our faith growth to the ways God helps the seeds grow into productive plants. Encourage the students to share their symbols and their meanings with others.

Bible readings: **Matthew 13:31–32; Galatians 2:16; Galatians 3:26**

Logical Deductions

Mara has six favorite Bible verses displayed on a bulletin board above her desk on colored cards: **Ephesians 2:8–9** (green); **Matthew 22:37–39** (green); **Isaiah 40:8** (yellow); **Romans 5:8** (blue); **Matthew 6:21** (red); **Psalm 37:4** (green).

Mara likes to keep these verses in a certain order. Use these clues and a Bible to place the verses in order on Mara's bulletin board below. Solution on page 62.

Clues

1. The verse about treasure and the verse about great commands are from the same book of the Bible but are not next to each other on the board and are not the same color.
2. The verse about flowers is below **Matthew 6:21**, and the verse on the blue card, but is above all the verses on green cards.
3. The longer Matthew verse is below one green card verse and **Isaiah 40:8**, but is above the verse that has the word *grace* in it.
4. The verse at the top is printed on a red card.
5. **Psalm 37:4** is not next to the verse on the red card.

Mystery Word Search 4

(Based on **John 3:1–18**)
Solution on page 64.

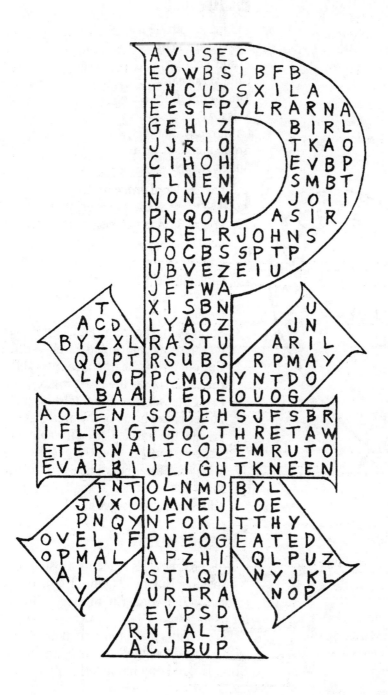

JOHN
NICODEMUS
JESUS
BORN
SPIRIT
WATER
LIGHT
BAPTIZE
RABBI
SON
ETERNAL
LIFE
LOVE

The Wonderful Mystery of God's Love Frame

Evidence

Old jigsaw puzzle pieces
Heavy cardboard
Poster board
Gold spray paint
Thick craft glue (Tacky)
Scissors
Calligraphy markers
Small pieces of yarn
Adhesive tape

FOR GOD SO LOVED THE WORLD . . .

John 3:16

Clues

1. Make a heart frame from the heavy cardboard using the pattern on page 49. Cut frames prior to class for younger students.
2. Glue puzzle pieces to the frame using the craft glue. Overlap pieces as needed to cover the entire frame.
3. Spray paint the frame and let it dry. Have an adult do the spray painting in a well-ventilated area.
4. Cut out a solid heart shape from the poster board, the same size as the heart frame.
5. Print the words of **John 3:16** on the center of the poster board heart in the area that will be uncovered by the frame. Use calligraphy markers to add a special touch.
6. Glue the poster board heart to the back of the heart frame. Attach a small piece of yarn with adhesive tape to serve as a hanger.

Deductions

This project gives students a visual reminder of the "Gospel in a Nutshell" (**John 3:16**). The puzzle pieces symbolize the wonderful mystery of God's great love for us in Jesus.

Let students make more than one frame to share with a friend, neighbor, homebound person, new Christian, nursing home resident, or hospital patient.

Gumshoe Rhyme Time

Use the clues to discover two rhyming words that describe the clue in a simpler way. The first one is done to help you get started. (The numbers in parentheses behind each clue indicate the number of syllables found in each of the words in the two-word rhyme.) Solution on page 62.

1. A church tower made of humans. (2) *people-steeple*

2. A shake of the Lord's head. (1) _____-_____

3. A floating bunch of rain water happy to be there when Jesus rose into heaven.(1)

   _____-_____

4. The unit used to determine the value of a chest of gold. (2) _____-

   _____

5. Green plants growing on the place of Jesus' death. (1)_____-_____

6. Set of steps on which you might talk to God. (1)_____-_____

7. What Jesus wore when He came alive again. (2 and 1)_____-_____

8. Time in heaven with God forever. (3) _____-_____

9. A container in which to keep God's free gift. (1)_____-_____

10. Forgiveness offered in Adam and Eve's first home. (2)_____-_____

Stained-Glass Treasures

Evidence

Makit-Bakit crystals (about 3–4 Tablespoons per student)
3″ wooden embroidery hoops (one for every two students)
Eye screws
Nature treasures (seeds, small flower petals, other flat items)
Flat wooden toothpicks (two per student)
Glue
Scissors
Flat cookie sheets
Aluminum foil
Tweezers
Oven
Ribbon scraps
Suction cup hooks for hanging (*optional*)

Clues

1. Preheat the oven to 375 degrees.
2. Cover the cookie sheets carefully with aluminum foil. Make sure the foil is completely smooth and has no crinkles.
3. Take the embroidery hoop apart to have two hoops. Tighten the one with the screw completely shut. Give each child one hoop.
4. Place the hoops on the cookie sheet so that they are lying flat. Arrange the nature treasures you have decorated inside the hoop. *Or* make a toothpick cross to lay in the center of the hoop. Glue one toothpick horizontally across another whole toothpick.
5. Carefully sprinkle the baking crystals inside the hoops. Try to avoid bumping the hoops so that crystals do not fall outside the hoops. Make sure the crystals go to the edges of the hoops. These should be layered at least two-deep. Several colors of crystals can be used together. Make sure the hoops lie flat on the cookie sheets and are not on top of the crystals before baking.
6. Place in a 375-degree oven and bake for about 10 minutes. Check the hoops for any spots without crystals. Add a few crystals with tweezers to cover any gaps as necessary. Then bake an additional 15 minutes. Check periodically. When the plastic is

relatively smooth, remove from the oven to cool. The crystals will give off an odor as they bake. Use these in a well-ventilated area according to package instructions. Be sure to have adult supervision with the baking process.
7. The plastic will cool within a few minutes. As it does, you'll hear a cracking sound. Remove the baked creations carefully from the foil. Gently peel off any foil from the melted plastic.
8. Place an eye screw in the top of any hoops that do not have a screw at the top. Make small bows with ribbon scraps and glue one to the top of each hoop.

Deductions

As you view the plastic creations hanging in a well-lighted window, pray a prayer to thank God for the beauty of His creation or for Jesus (if you made treasures with toothpick crosses). These make excellent gifts to share with homebound people or people in nursing homes.

Mystery Word Search 5

(Based on **Matthew 13:44**)
Solution on page 64.

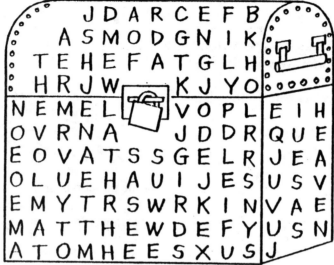

```
J D A R C E F B
A S M O D G N I K
T E H E F A T G L H
H R J W   K J Y O
N E M E L   V O P L E I H
O V R N A   J D D R Q U E
E O V A T S S G E L R J E A
O L U E H A U I J E S U S V
E M Y T R S W R K I N V A E
M A T T H E W D E F Y U S N
A T O M H E E S X U S J
```

M A T T H E W
F I E L D
T R E A S U R E
K I N G D O M
H E A V E N
J O Y
S H A R E
J E S U S
L O V E

Treasure Symbol Discovery

Clues

1. Design a symbol based on one of the Bible stories from VBS on the drawing paper.
2. Transfer the design to the sandpaper using crayons. Be sure to press firmly and to color darkly.
3. Turn the sandpaper colored-side down onto a piece of white copier paper. Place both items on top of a pile of newspaper.
4. Iron the backside of the sandpaper with a medium-hot iron for 10 seconds. The heat will cause the crayon on the sandpaper to melt on the copier paper, thus causing the design to transfer. **An adult should do all ironing**.
5. Remove sandpaper from copier paper immediately.

Evidence

Drawing paper
Medium-grade sandpaper
Crayons
Lightweight white copier paper
Iron
Newspaper

Deductions

Talk about the meaning of the Christian symbols together as a class. Let willing students explain the meaning of any symbols they have developed.

Use the designs on Christian greeting cards to share with friends or homebound members of your congregation. Or print Bible verses on the backside of the design papers to help reinforce verses learned.

God Has Found Me Bulletin Board

3↟

Evidence

Construction paper
Nontoxic, washable dark-colored ink pad
Tacks or staples

Clues

1. Cut out a picture of Detective Evan Dense from construction paper based on the drawing shown here. Staple Detective Dense to the left-hand side of the bulletin board.
2. Cut out letters to spell **GOD HAS FOUND ME!** and staple these across the top of the bulletin board.
3. Cut out a 4″ diameter construction paper circle for each child. Label the bottom of each circle with a child's name. Include a circle for yourself and for each of your classroom helpers as well.
4. When children arrive on the first day, have them print their thumbprint on their circle. Hang these on the bulletin board. On each of the following days, have them add the print of another finger: index finger—second day, middle finger—third day, and so on.

Special Agent Clue Holders

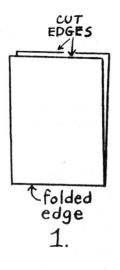

CUT EDGES

folded edge

1.

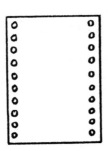

2.

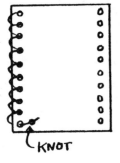

KNOT

3.

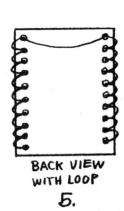

BACK VIEW WITH LOOP

5.

Special Agent

Jane

FRONT VIEW   KNOT

4.

Evidence

One 4½″ × 11″ rectangle of leather-look vinyl per student (available at craft stores)
24″ length of leather lacing
Hole punch
Permanent markers or fabric paints
3″ × 5″ pads of paper (one per student)

Clues

1. Fold the vinyl rectangle in half with the wrong sides facing in. The folded size of the vinyl is now 4½″ × 5½″. See Illustration 1.
2. Punch 10 holes along each 5½″ side, taking care to space the holes evenly and to punch through both folded parts of the fabric. See Illustration 2.
3. Beginning at the bottom hole on the left-hand side of the fabric, pull the leather lacing through this hole about 2″. Knot this end of the lacing. Continue lacing through the holes on this side of the fabric using a whip stitch. See Illustration 3.
4. When you reach the top of the left-hand side, leave about 3″ of lacing across the back of the fabric. Then proceed down the right-hand side of the fabric, once again going through the holes using a whip stitch. When you reach the bottom of the right-hand side, knot the end of the lacing to complete the stitching. See Illustration 4.
5. Decorate the front of the vinyl holder you have made with permanent markers or fabric paints. Use Christians symbols such as hearts and crosses along with the words *Special Agent*. Students may also wish to print their names in a lower corner of the holder.
6. When the design is dry, place the pad of paper inside the holder. Now the young sleuths are ready to do some detective work!

Deductions

Students may wish to write each day's Bible verse on the pad inside the holder. They also can keep special Bible messages or a small picture of Jesus inside the holder. Encourage the students to share these items with others when VBS is over.

Agent Reminder
Board Magnet

Evidence

One minichalkboard per student (2" × 3", available
   at craft stores)
Two thin craft sticks per student
Scissors
Felt or fun foam
Thick craft glue
One 3" self-adhesive magnet strip per student

Clues

1. Make a cross using the craft sticks. Cut one stick
   and glue it to serve as the cross bar on the other
   stick. Glue the finished cross to the right-hand
   side of the chalkboard as shown in the illustration.
2. Decorate the board with a message or symbol cut
   from the felt or fun foam. Use crosses, hearts,
   open Bibles, magnifying glasses, and other symbols to make reminders of God's love. Glue the
   symbols to the center area of the chalkboard.
3. Stick the magnet strip across the back of the
   chalkboard to use as a refrigerator magnet.

Deductions

   This craft would work well to summarize a student's
VBS experience. Help the students develop a symbol or
picture that reminds them not only of God's great love
for them, but also about their greatest treasure, Jesus.
These magnets could also serve as reminders that God
gives us the desire to continue to be detectives of His
Word throughout our entire lives.

Mystery Appearing Puzzle

1	2	3	4	5	6
7	8	🖐	11	12	13
14	15	16	17	18	🛏 f

Evidence

One large sheet white poster board
Markers
Tacks or masking tape
20 smaller pieces of paper (each the same size,
   enough to cover the poster board puzzle)
Adhesive tape

Clues

1. Enlarge the puzzle found on page 57 onto the poster board. You can also develop your own rebus Bible verse puzzle based on another of the verses your students have studied. Tack the finished puzzle to a bulletin board or tape it to a wall of your classroom at a level where it can be easily seen by your students.

2. Lightly tape the 20 small pieces of paper over the puzzle to cover it. Number the pieces of paper 1–20.

3. Let the students choose four numbers each day to slowly uncover the puzzle. Allow time for students to guess answers to the puzzle each day. Challenge your sleuths to discover the answer before day 5!

Deductions

This puzzle is an excellent way to review Bible verses and give the students some detective fun! **John 3:16** is a good verse to illustrate for an activity such as this.

Special Agent Footprints Bulletin Board or Banner

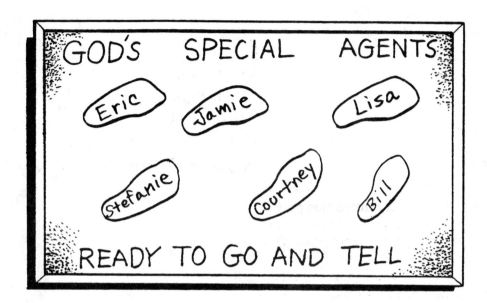

Evidence

For a Bulletin Board
Construction paper
Tacks or staples
Markers
Scissors

For a Banner
Butcher paper
Tempera paint
Shallow pan
Tub of water
Paper towels
Markers
Masking tape

Clues

For a Bulletin Board
1. Have each child stand with one sock-covered foot on a piece of construction paper. Trace around the student's foot with a pencil. Older students could take turns tracing one another's feet.
2. Cut out each footprint and label with the child's name.
3. Staple or tack the footprints to a bulletin board. Cut out letters for a caption: **GOD'S SPECIAL AGENTS—READY TO GO AND TELL.**

For a Banner
1. Cover your work area thoroughly with newspaper.
2. Premix tempera paint to a fairly thick consistency in a shallow pan. Place this paint mixture close to where you have spread out the butcher paper banner background.
3. Have each child take off his or her shoe and sock from one foot. Have the child dip his or her foot into the paint pan so that the bottom of the foot is covered with paint. Then have the child step and make a footprint on the banner paper.
4. Have clean water and paper towels ready so that the child can immediately clean his or her foot.
5. Print each child's name directly below his or her footprint.
6. Label the banner, **GOD'S SPECIAL AGENTS—READY TO GO AND TELL.**

Deductions

Use this bulletin board or banner activity as a great way to record the students in your VBS class. As you make the footprints, remind the students that God made each of them special. God uses each one of us in special ways to tell others the Good News about Jesus.

Name That Detective
Bulletin Board

Evidence

Construction paper
Scissors
Pencils
Markers
Tacks or staples

Clues

1. With a pencil, lightly print your name in large letters on a piece of construction paper.
2. Now draw a design around the outer edges of the shape formed by the letters in your name. See the illustration.
3. Cut out your name design, keeping it a one-piece shape. Gently erase the pencil lines within the shape that you originally made.
4. Using markers, write clue words that describe you on your name shape. Your clues could include your favorite food, hobby, sport, pet, friend, or toy.
5. Tack or staple the name shapes on a bulletin board. Cut out and place a caption such as **NAME THAT DETECTIVE** on the board.

Deductions

   Use this bulletin board idea as a get-acquainted activity for your students. If students' names cannot be identified by the outer shapes and clue words, trace the letters of their name clearly on their design so that the name can be easily seen.

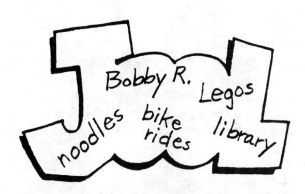

Bible Verse Discoveries

2. Encourage the students, as they work in large or small groups, to fill in the missing letters to complete the verse. You can also play this game in a "Wheel of Fortune" manner. Assign one point per vowel. If a team selects an "e" and there are eight of them in the puzzle, the team would be awarded eight points. The team with the most points when correctly guessing the puzzle wins.

Evidence

Chalkboard or large pieces of chart paper
Chalk or markers

Clues

1. Preprint on the chalkboard or large sheet of paper a Bible verse the students have studied, but leave out all the vowels. Where the vowels should be, leave blank spaces. *For older students, selected consonants could be left out.*

Deductions

Use portions of the Apostles' Creed or the Lord's Prayer as well (if your students are familiar with them). This activity is another way students can review Bible verses and Christian truths using detective and puzzle-solving skills.

F_R G_D S_ L_V_D TH_ W_RLD TH_T H_ G_V_ H_S _N_ _ND _NLY S_N, TH_T WH__V_R B_L__V_S _N H_M SH_LL N_T P_R_SH B_T H_V_ _T_RN_L L_F_. J_HN 3:16

is awarded this certificate for being a SUPER SLEUTH! May God give you the
continued desire to study His Word so that you may know Him better and better!

_____

(Date)

_____

(Teacher)

For God so loved the world that He gave His one and
only Son, that whoever believes in Him shall not perish
but have eternal life.   John 3:16

Puzzle Solutions

Logical Deductions (p. 46)

Correct order (from top):

1. Matthew 6:21
2. Romans 5:8
3. Isaiah 40:8
4. Psalm 37:4
5. Matthew 22:37–39
6. Ephesians 2:8–9

Gumshoe Rhyme Time (p. 50)

1. People-steeple
2. God-nod
3. Proud-cloud
4. Treasure-measure
5. Cross-moss
6. Prayer-stairs
7. Arose-clothes
8. Salvation-vacation
9. Grace-vase
10. Garden-pardon

Mystery Word Search 1 (pg. 15)

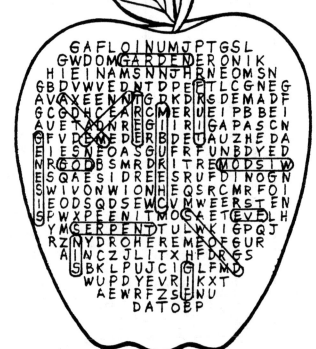

Mystery Word Search 2 (pg. 25)

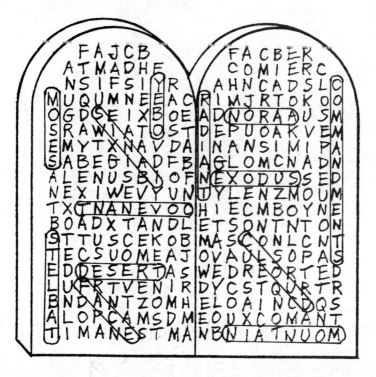

Mystery Word Search 3 (pg. 38)

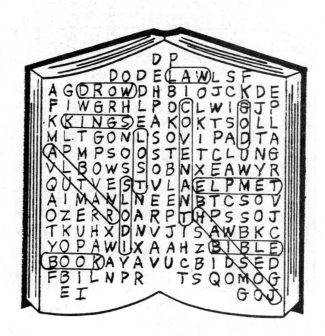

Mystery Word Search 4 (pg. 47)

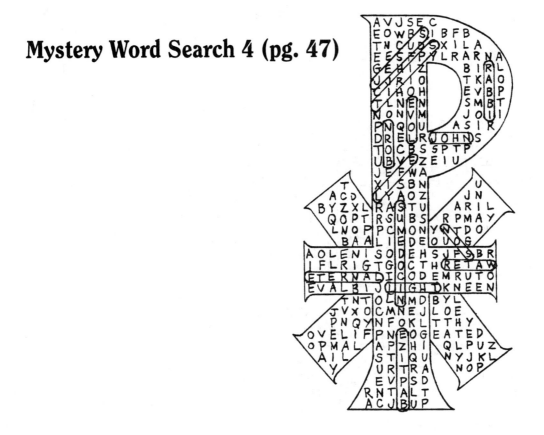

Mystery Word Search 5 (pg. 52)

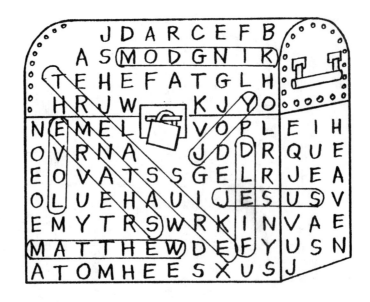